CW00498699

LOS ANGELE

GUIDE 2023

The Ultimate Pocket Guide to Discovering the Glamour, Culture, Unique Neighborhoods, and Experiences in the City of Dreams. All You Need to Know for a Memorable Trip

ETHAN FOX

COPYRIGHT

TABLE OF CONTENTS

WELCOME TO LOS ANGELES

Los Angeles, sometimes known as LA, is a bustling and diversified metropolis in Southern California, United States. It serves as a worldwide hub for entertainment, culture, commerce, and tourism as the biggest city in California and the second-most populated city in the United States. Los Angeles, which covers an area of roughly 1,302 square kilometers (502 square miles), is recognized for its magnificent coastline, lovely weather, and famous structures.

Why you should visit Los Angeles

Visiting Los Angeles is a once-in-a-lifetime opportunity. Here are a few reasons why you should visit this beautiful city:

a. Entertainment Capital: Hollywood, the world-famous film and television business, is headquartered in Los Angeles, the global entertainment capital. Visitors may tour iconic studios, attend film premieres, and stroll along the legendary Hollywood Walk of Fame.

b. Cultural Diversity: Los Angeles has a strong multicultural background, with communities from all over the world contributing to its eclectic fabric. LA provides a diverse range of cultural experiences and gastronomic delights, from the thriving Latino districts of Boyle Heights and Olvera Street to the vibrant Korean community of Koreatown.

c. Iconic Landmarks: The city is dotted with iconic landmarks that have come to represent American culture. Visitors may absorb the spirit of Los Angeles through its renowned architecture and sights, which range from the famed Hollywood Sign to the majestic Griffith Observatory.

d. Natural Beauty: Los Angeles is surrounded by stunning natural surroundings. Outdoor enthusiasts may enjoy hiking, surfing, and other recreational activities on its beautiful beaches, including Santa Monica and Venice Beach, as well as neighboring picturesque areas such as Griffith Park and the Santa Monica Mountains.

e. Museums & Art: The city is a mecca for art lovers, with world-class institutions such as The Getty Center, the Los Angeles County Museum of Art (LACMA), and the Museum of Contemporary Art (MOCA) to choose from. These cultural institutions hold world-class collections and present exhibitions that celebrate art in all of its forms.

History and Cultural Relevance

Los Angeles has an interesting past that adds to its cultural relevance. The area was originally inhabited by the Tongva and Chumash Native American tribes before being invaded by the Spanish in the 18th century and becoming part of Mexico in 1821. Following the Mexican-American War, the Treaty of Guadalupe Hidalgo in 1848 gave the area to the United States, paving the way for the city of Los Angeles to be established in 1850.

Los Angeles has seen incredible expansion and transformation throughout its history. The discovery of oil and the rise of the entertainment sector spurred the city's fast expansion in the early twentieth century. The advent of Hollywood and the creation of major film studios cemented Los Angeles' position as the world's entertainment hub.

Los Angeles was also important in the civil rights struggle. During the Chicano and African American civil rights movements of the 1960s and 1970s, the city was a hotbed of agitation. Activists such as Cesar Chavez and Dolores Huerta pushed for farmworker rights, and luminaries such as Martin Luther King Jr. and Malcolm X delivered powerful speeches in the city.

Los Angeles is increasingly recognized for its cultural achievements and progressive attitudes. It promotes variety, embraces many creative forms, and uses its entertainment sector to create popular culture. The city's influence reaches well beyond its borders, influencing fashion, music, and lifestyle trends all over the world.

To summarize, Los Angeles is a vibrant and culturally significant city that provides tourists with a wide range of experiences. From its bustling entertainment sector to its varied neighborhoods and natural beauty, Los Angeles captivates visitors of all ages.

PLANNING YOUR TRIP

Geographical Location

Los Angeles is located in Southern California, on the Pacific Coast, and is bounded to the west by the Pacific Ocean. It is bounded to the north by the Santa Monica Mountains, to the east by the San Gabriel Mountains, and to the south by the Los Angeles River and Long Beach. The city is located in Los

Angeles County, which encompasses a large territory and numerous smaller cities and settlements.

Best Time to Visit

Los Angeles has a Mediterranean climate with moderate, rainy winters and warm, dry summers. The city has reasonably consistent and pleasant weather throughout the year, making it a popular tourist destination.

a. Winter (December to February): Average temperatures in Los Angeles range from 10°C to 20°C (50°F to 68°F). Rain showers are typical during this time of year, although they are usually short. If you prefer milder weather and fewer visitors, winter is a terrific time to come.

b. Spring (March to May): Spring weather in Los Angeles is temperate and pleasant, with temperatures ranging from 15°C to 25°C (59°F to 77°F). The city is covered with brightly blooming flowers, and it's a fantastic time to see outdoor sites and attend numerous events and festivals.

c. Summer (June to August): Temperatures in Los Angeles range from 20°C to 30°C (68°F to 86°F). Because of the beautiful weather and school vacations, this is the busiest season for tourists in the city. It's the perfect season for beach activities and outdoor exploring.

d. Fall (September to November): Temperatures in Los Angeles range from 15°C to 25°C (59°F to 77°F). The weather continues to be beautiful, and the tourist throngs begin to dwindle. Fall is an excellent season to engage in outdoor activities, see sites, and attend cultural events.

It's worth noting that Los Angeles may occasionally endure heatwaves, especially during the summer. During hot weather, it's best to remain hydrated, use sunscreen, and take all required measures.

Overall, the ideal time to visit Los Angeles is determined by your choices and the activities you want to pursue. Spring and fall are popular travel seasons due to their nicer weather and fewer tourists. However, because of the city's nice temperature, Los Angeles can be enjoyed all year.

Getting to LA

- Airports: Several airports serve Los Angeles, with Los Angeles International Airport

(LAX) serving as the principal international and domestic gateway. LAX is one of the busiest airports in the world, with several airline options. Other airports in the area include Hollywood Burbank Airport (BUR) and Long Beach Airport (LGB), both of which mostly serve domestic flights.

- Public Transportation: Los Angeles has an extensive public transit system that includes buses, light rail, and subway services. The Metro Bus and Metro Rail services are operated by the Los Angeles County Metropolitan Transportation Authority (Metro), and they provide quick and economical transportation across the city and nearby areas. Furthermore, DASH (Downtown Area Short Hop) buses service certain communities around the city.

- Highway: The city of Los Angeles has a complex network of roads and freeways that link various regions of the city and beyond. Interstate 5 (I-5), Interstate 10 (I-10), and Interstate 405 (I-405) are some of the important freeways. However, during peak hours, traffic congestion may be a major concern, so it's critical to arrange your travel times properly.

Currency, Language, and Safety Tips

- Local Currency: The US Dollar (USD) is the official currency of the United States. ATMs are extensively available across Los Angeles, and the vast majority of businesses take credit cards. It is a good idea to notify your bank of your trip intentions to avoid any problems with using your cards while in the city.

- Language: English is the most widely spoken language in Los Angeles. Due to its varied population, though, you may discover individuals speaking a variety of languages, including Spanish, Korean, Chinese, and others. Because most signs and information in the city are in English, having a basic grasp of the language will assist you navigate the city.

Safety Recommendations

a. As in any major city, it's critical to be aware of your surroundings and take standard steps to keep your valuables secure.
b. Avoid going alone at night in unfamiliar or poorly lit locations, especially in regions notorious for high crime rates.

c. Licensed and respected transportation options, such as official taxis, ride-sharing apps, or public transit, should be used.

d. When using ATMs in public locations, practice caution and attempt to utilize machines in safe and well-lit areas.

e. Be aware of the ocean currents and heed lifeguard directions when visiting the beach for your safety.

f. In the event of an emergency, phone 911 for urgent help.

Overall, Los Angeles is a safe city for tourists, however, using common sense and being aware of your surroundings will improve your trip. Interacting with locals and obtaining guidance from hotel employees or tourism information centers may also give useful insights and safety suggestions unique to your planned activities and places.

NEIGHBORHOODS AND ATTRACTIONS

Hollywood

One of the first locations that people think of when they think of Los Angeles is Hollywood. Hollywood, known as the world's entertainment center, is a renowned area rich in history, glamor, and glamor. It has been the worldwide film and television industry's epicenter for almost a century, attracting people from all over the world. Here are some of the finest places to see in Hollywood, ranging from the renowned Walk of Fame to the breathtaking vistas of the Hollywood Sign.

Walk of Fame

The Hollywood Walk of Fame is one of the world's most renowned pathways. The Walk of Fame, which runs for 1.3 miles along Hollywood Boulevard and Vine Street, is adorned with over 2,690 brass stars, each holding the name of a significant personality from the entertainment business. These stars are given to actors, artists, directors, producers, and other notable people who have made major contributions to the entertainment industry. As you walk along the Walk of Fame, you'll find yourself surrounded by the names of Hollywood superstars, producing a sense of wonder and veneration for the industry's history.

TCL Chinese Theatre

The TCL Chinese Theatre, formerly known as Grauman's Chinese Theatre, is a Hollywood landmark. The Forecourt of the luminaries, a part of the theater entrance that includes hundreds of handprints, footprints, and autographs of Hollywood luminaries, is historically significant. This custom dates back to 1927 when actress Norma Talmadge inadvertently walked into wet pavement during the premiere of the film "The King of Kings."

Visitors may view new movie releases on the huge screen inside the cinema, which has a spectacular Chinese-inspired interior design. The TCL Chinese Theatre has held several film premieres and events, making it a must-see for any film buff visiting Hollywood.

Hollywood Sign

The Hollywood Sign is undoubtedly Los Angeles' most recognizable emblem. The sign, perched atop Mount Lee in the Hollywood Hills, was originally spelled "Hollywoodland" and advertised a real estate development in the 1920s. It has become a symbol of the city's entertainment sector as well as a global depiction of Hollywood's popularity and attraction over the years.

The sign may be viewed from a variety of locations across the city, but the finest views are from Griffith Observatory and the hiking trails in Griffith Park. Guided tours are offered to take tourists near the sign for a closer look, affording wonderful picture opportunities and insights into its history.

Downtown Los Angeles

Downtown Los Angeles, often known as DTLA, is the city's primary commercial sector and a cultural powerhouse that has seen a significant revival in recent years. Downtown Los Angeles, with its combination of historic structures, modern architecture, and bustling street life, provides a varied choice of attractions for tourists to explore. From world-class art at The Broad to the bustling Grand Central Market, here are some of the top attractions that make Downtown Los Angeles a must-see.

The Broad

The Broad is a contemporary art museum on Grand Avenue in Downtown Los Angeles that opened in 2015. It houses an excellent collection of modern and contemporary art from the 1950s to the present. The structure itself is a piece of art, with a distinctive honeycomb-like outside design.

Inside, visitors may admire pieces by Andy Warhol, Jeff Koons, Jean-Michel Basquiat, and Yayoi Kusama, among others. Although general admission is free, previous reservations are encouraged to secure entrance. The Broad is not just a refuge for art lovers, but it is also a cultural icon that has become an important element of the Downtown LA art scene.

Grand Central Market

Grand Central Market, located on Broadway in Downtown Los Angeles, is a historic culinary marketplace that was established in 1917 and has been a gathering spot for locals and visitors alike for over a century. The market is home to a vast assortment of food vendors with cuisines ranging from Mexican and Thai to Italian and Mediterranean.

Visitors may browse the busy aisles and sample delectable meals from numerous vendors. Whether you're hungry for tacos, pupusas, ramen, or gourmet coffee, Grand Central Market offers something for everyone. The market also serves as a platform for budding local chefs and food entrepreneurs, contributing to the city's lively and ever-changing culinary culture.

Walt Disney Concert Hall

The Walt Disney Concert Hall, designed by architect Frank Gehry, is an architectural marvel and home of the Los Angeles Philharmonic. This magnificent venue on Grand Avenue is known for its striking stainless steel facade that reflects the surrounding cityscape. Orchestral concerts, recitals, and guest appearances by world-class musicians are all held at the concert hall.

Even if you aren't going to a concert, you should go to the Walt Disney Concert Hall. Explore the inside of the landmark edifice, including the auditorium and the lovely garden terrace, on a guided tour. The music hall exemplifies the city's devotion to the arts and pays homage to one of its most beloved innovators, Walt Disney.

Union Station

Union Station in Downtown Los Angeles is a historic transit hub that mixes architectural splendor with a look into the city's past. The station's beautiful combination of Spanish Colonial Revival and Art Deco styles, built in 1939, has made it an iconic monument. When you enter, you'll be taken back to the golden age of rail travel.

Walk into the exquisite waiting room, which is decorated with intricate tile work and genuine historical elements. Union Station also has several food options, including both premium and informal establishments. The station is a key transit hub for trains and Metro lines, giving it an easy way to get to Downtown Los Angeles.

Exploring Downtown Los Angeles provides an opportunity to learn about the city's rich history, architectural marvels, and gastronomic pleasures. There is something for everyone in this lively and ever-changing area, from modern art at The Broad to the thriving culinary scene at Grand Central Market. Downtown Los Angeles' rebirth has transformed it into a dynamic cultural attraction that should not be missed during your visit to the city.

Santa Monica

Santa Monica is a picturesque beachside community on the western fringe of Los Angeles County that offers a laid-back coastal ambiance with a dynamic mix of entertainment, shopping, and outdoor activities. Here are some of the major attractions that make Santa Monica a must-visit location, ranging from the renowned Santa Monica Pier to the bustling Third Street Promenade and the picturesque Santa Monica State Beach.

Santa Monica Pier

The Santa Monica Pier is a well-known landmark that has entertained both locals and visitors for more than a century. The pier, which stretches out into the Pacific Ocean, provides beautiful views of the coastline and acts as a focus of entertainment and relaxation. The Pacific Park amusement park, with its Ferris wheel and roller coaster, is one of the pier's many attractions.

Take a trip on the Ferris wheel for a bird's-eye view of the city and the ocean, or put your abilities to the test at the carnival games and arcade. The ancient carousel, which has been entertaining guests since

1922, is also housed on the pier. There are also a variety of eating options available, ranging from informal seafood stalls to sit-down restaurants, making it an ideal location for a fun-filled day at the beach.

Third Street Promenade

The Third Street Promenade, located in the center of Santa Monica, is a busy pedestrian-only shopping and entertainment zone. This vibrant boulevard, lined with a mix of retail outlets, restaurants, cafés, and street entertainers, provides a unique mixture of local and international businesses.

Stroll down the busy street, peruse the stores, and sample the many gastronomic offers. The Santa Monica Place Mall, an open-air retail area with premium stores and eating options, is also located on the Third Street Promenade. The Third Street Promenade has something for everyone, whether you're seeking the newest fashion trends or a one-of-a-kind keepsake.

Santa Monica State Beach

Santa Monica State Beach, which stretches three miles along the Pacific Ocean, is a popular location for both locals and visitors. It provides a classic Southern California beach experience with its vast sandy beachfront, stunning vistas, and bustling beach culture.

The beach offers several chances for pleasure and relaxation. Relax on the sand, take a refreshing plunge in the sea, or simply enjoy the sunshine. The beach also has picnic spaces, volleyball courts, and bike routes, allowing guests to participate in a variety of activities.

Rent a bicycle or rollerblades and cruise down the Marvin Braude Bike Trail, popularly known as "The Strand," which spans along the shoreline for a more active experience. You may also access the Santa Monica Pier and its attractions from the beach, offering a smooth transition between the sandy beachfront and the vibrant entertainment district.

Santa Monica has a distinct combination of beachfront charm, shopping pleasures, and energetic entertainment. Santa Monica has something for everyone, whether you want to spend a calm day on the beach, explore fashionable stores and boutiques, or enjoy the dynamic street scene. Santa Monica, with its stunning coastline and energetic environment, is a must-see for anybody looking for the traditional California beach experience.

Beverly Hills

Beverly Hills is a wealthy city in the center of Los Angeles. It is well-known for its glamorous reputation and luxurious lifestyle, and it provides a one-of-a-kind combination of wealth, beauty, and cultural attractions. Here are some of the top attractions that make Beverly Hills a must-visit location, ranging from the iconic Rodeo Drive to the historic Greystone Mansion and the gorgeous Getty Center.

Rodeo Drive

Rodeo Drive is linked with luxury shopping and is one of the world's most recognized avenues. It is a shopper's paradise, lined with high-end designer stores, luxury brands, and superb jewelers. Rodeo Drive offers the greatest in fashion, accessories, and jewelry, from Gucci and Chanel to Prada and Louis Vuitton.

Even if you aren't seeking to splurge on luxury things, a stroll down Rodeo Drive is an unforgettable experience. Immerse yourself in the grandeur and elegance of this historic boulevard, observe the stunning stores, and soak in the opulent ambiance that pervades the region.

Greystone Mansion

Greystone Mansion, also known as Doheny Mansion, is a historic home amid Beverly Hills' hills.

This majestic palace, built in 1927, is an architectural marvel and a window into the city's past. The house provides a calm getaway from the bustling streets below, surrounded by beautifully planted gardens and affording panoramic views of the city.

Visitors may explore the grounds and join guided tours to learn about the mansion's history and significance. Greystone Mansion's interior has been featured in several films and television series, adding to its attraction and beauty. A visit to Greystone Mansion is a must for anybody interested in history, architecture, or simply seeking a tranquil refuge.

The Getty Center

While officially located in adjacent Brentwood, The Getty Center is easily accessible from Beverly Hills and is a cultural monument not to be missed. This architectural wonder, perched on a mountaintop above the city, displays a large collection of European paintings, sculptures, and decorative arts.

The remarkable collection of the Getty Center contains works by notable painters such as Van Gogh, Rembrandt, Monet, and Renoir. Aside from the art, the facility features amazing city vistas, well-groomed gardens, and stunning buildings built by Richard Meier.

Visitors can explore the galleries, relax in the serene outdoor settings, and participate in the center's educational activities and events. The Getty Center is not just a paradise for art connoisseurs, but also a cultural institution that offers all visitors a unique and enlightening experience.

Beverly Hills has become an iconic destination due to its sense of wealth and elegance. This city exudes luxury and indulgence, from the premium shopping on Rodeo Drive to the historic beauty of Greystone

Mansion and the artistic riches of The Getty Center. A trip to Beverly Hills allows you to immerse yourself in the glittering world of Hollywood's elite while also experiencing the charm of this world-famous area.

The Venice Beach

Venice Beach is a bustling and colorful area on Los Angeles' westside. It provides a unique combination of beach culture, street art, and energetic entertainment and is known for its bohemian vibe, colorful murals, and renowned boardwalk. The busy Venice Boardwalk, Muscle Beach, and the stylish stores on Abbot Kinney Boulevard are just a few of the major attractions that make Venice Beach a must-see trip.

Venice Boardwalk

Venice Beach's heart and soul is the Venice Boardwalk, commonly known as the Ocean Front Walk. This busy pedestrian promenade runs the length of the beach for two and a half miles and is packed with stores, restaurants, street performers, and artists. The Venice Boardwalk is a dynamic and varied environment that embodies the creative and free-spirited attitude of the city.

Along the boardwalk, you'll come across a variety of street sellers offering artwork, jewelry, apparel, and souvenirs. Enjoy the exciting environment, live music performances, and diverse street performers displaying their skills. The boardwalk is also a terrific area to people-watch and absorb the colorful spirit of this one-of-a-kind community.

Muscle Beach

Muscle Beach is a renowned outdoor gym and fitness playground located at the southern end of the Venice Beach Recreation Center. It was founded in the 1930s as a training facility for bodybuilders and fitness aficionados, and it has since become a symbol of Southern California's fitness culture.

On the rings, bars, and other equipment, visitors may witness experienced athletes and bodybuilders execute spectacular acrobatics, weightlifting, and gymnastics. Muscle Beach is not just a location to see fitness fanatics, but it is also a public environment where people of all fitness levels may exercise. If you're feeling brave, you can even participate in a fitness class or try out the equipment for yourself.

Abbot Kinney Boulevard

Abbot Kinney Boulevard, also known as the "coolest block in America," is a trendy street in the heart of Venice. It has become a mecca for fashionistas, foodies, and art enthusiasts since it is lined with chic boutiques, hip cafés, art galleries, and one-of-a-kind stores.

Explore the unique mix of businesses, which includes local designers, vintage apparel, and one-of-a-kind finds. Enjoy a cup of coffee at one of the fashionable cafés, gourmet food, or handcrafted ice cream. Abbot Kinney Boulevard is also well-known for its lively nightlife, with several clubs and live music venues that come alive after dark.

Aside from shopping and dining, Abbot Kinney Boulevard is home to several art galleries displaying modern works by local and worldwide artists. Take a stroll along the avenue, immerse yourself in the creative ambiance, and explore all that Venice Beach has to offer in terms of creativity.

Venice Beach is an enthralling community that values individualism, creativity, and a relaxed beach lifestyle. It provides a varied selection of activities that fully define the character of this distinctive coastal city, from the vibrant Venice Boardwalk to the workout paradise of Muscle Beach and the stylish stores on Abbot Kinney Boulevard. A visit to Venice Beach allows you to immerse yourself in the colorful and bohemian atmosphere that has made it a popular destination for both locals and visitors.

Griffith Observatory

Griffith Park is a large urban park in Los Angeles that is located in the eastern section of the Santa Monica Mountains. It is one of the largest urban parks in North America, spanning over 4,300 acres, and provides a variety of recreational activities, natural beauty, and cultural attractions. Here are some of the major attractions that make Griffith Park a must-see trip, ranging from the renowned Griffith Observatory to the Griffith Park Zoo and Botanical Gardens.

Griffith Observatory

The Griffith Observatory, perched on the southern slope of Mount Hollywood, is an architectural marvel and a Los Angeles landmark. It was built in 1935 and provides breathtaking views of the city skyline, the Pacific Ocean, and the surrounding mountains. The observatory is dedicated to public astronomy and offers visitors a variety of exhibitions, planetarium performances, and telescopes to explore and learn about the cosmos.

Visitors may take guided tours of the facilities, participate in educational events and live presentations, and even look through telescopes at celestial objects. Hiking routes connect to panoramic overlooks at the Griffith Observatory, allowing visitors to combine their passion for astronomy with the beauty of nature.

Griffith Park Observatory

Not to be confused with the Griffith Observatory, the Griffith Park Observatory is another prominent attraction inside the park. It is a historic observatory that was before the contemporary Griffith Observatory. Built-in 1912, it performed a significant role in furthering scientific research and public education about astronomy.

While the old observatory is no longer in use, visitors may explore the historic structure and learn about its significance in the study of astronomy. The Griffith Park Observatory gives a fascinating view into the park's rich history and the evolution of astronomical knowledge in Los Angeles.

Los Angeles Zoo and Botanical Gardens

The Los Angeles Zoo and Botanical Gardens, located inside Griffith Park, is a family-friendly destination featuring a vast assortment of wildlife and plant species. The zoo, which houses over 1,400 animals from all over the world, offers a unique opportunity to view and learn about numerous species in realistic environments.

Visitors may walk around the zoo's exhibits, which include the Rainforest of the Americas, Elephants of Asia, and Australia. The botanical gardens include a large plant collection, including rare and endangered species. Throughout the year, the zoo also provides interactive experiences, educational programs, and special events, making it an entertaining and instructive destination for people of all ages.

Griffith Park contains a wealth of natural beauty, cultural value, and recreational activities. A visit to Griffith Park is an unforgettable experience that showcases the best of nature and culture in Los Angeles, whether you're exploring the wonders of the universe at the Griffith Observatory, delving into the park's rich history at the Griffith Park Observatory, or immersing yourself in the diverse wildlife at the Los Angeles Zoo and Botanical Gardens.

CULTURAL EXPERIENCES

Museum of Contemporary Art (MOCA)

Located in Downtown Los Angeles, the Museum of Contemporary Art (MOCA) is dedicated to showcasing contemporary art from around the world. With its mission to collect, preserve, and present groundbreaking artworks, MOCA has established itself as a leading institution in the field of contemporary art.

MOCA's collection encompasses a wide range of mediums, including painting, sculpture, photography, video, and installation art. The museum has a particular focus on post-1940s art movements and is known for its commitment to showcasing works by emerging and underrepresented artists.

Visitors to MOCA can explore thought-provoking exhibitions that challenge traditional notions of art and engage with current social and cultural issues. The museum also hosts educational programs, talks, and performances that further enrich the visitor experience and provide opportunities for dialogue and engagement.

MOCA has three locations: MOCA Grand Avenue, MOCA Geffen, and MOCA Pacific Design Center. Each venue offers a unique perspective on contemporary art and provides a platform for artists to experiment and push the boundaries of artistic expression.

Music and Entertainment

Los Angeles is a creative and innovative hotspot, not just in the visual arts but also in music and entertainment. The city has a dynamic music culture that appeals to a wide spectrum of preferences, from renowned venues to legendary concert halls. Here are the top three music and entertainment places in Los Angeles.

Hollywood Bowl

The Hollywood Bowl is a well-known outdoor amphitheater in the Hollywood Hills. It is one of the world's most famous concert venues, thanks to its unique bandshell and gorgeous environment. Orchestral concerts, popular music concerts, film screenings with live orchestra accompaniment, and cultural events are all held at the Bowl.

Attending a performance at the Hollywood Bowl is a must-do in Los Angeles. Visitors are welcome to bring picnic baskets and dine beneath the stars while watching world-class musicians play on the stage. The acoustics and open-air ambiance of the arena create a magnificent environment that adds to the attractiveness of the performances.

The Troubadour

The Troubadour is a famed West Hollywood music venue. Since its inception in 1957, the Troubadour has played an important part in molding the careers of several musicians, including Elton John, Joni Mitchell, and James Taylor, who all performed there early in their careers.

The Troubadour's small location allows for an up-close and personal encounter with the musicians. Visitors may enjoy concerts by both new and renowned performers from various genres such as rock, folk, indie, and alternative.

The Troubadour's rich history and intimate setting make it a popular choice for music fans looking for a genuine and unforgettable live music experience.

The Roxy Theatre

The Roxy Theatre, located on the Sunset Strip in West Hollywood, is another legendary venue that has been a fixture of the Los Angeles music industry since its inception in 1973. The Roxy, known for its dynamic atmosphere and varied roster, has featured great performers such as Bruce Springsteen, David Bowie, and Guns N' Roses.

The venue continues to feature known and upcoming acts from a variety of genres, including rock, pop, hip-hop, and electronic music. The Roxy's compact environment offers an immersive experience, allowing music fans to sense the energy and connection between the artists and the crowd.

The Roxy, in addition to hosting music performances, also offers comedy shows and other events, enhancing its status as a cultural destination in Los Angeles.

The music and entertainment industry in Los Angeles is as broad and vibrant as the city itself. Whether you're looking for a wonderful night beneath the stars at the Hollywood Bowl, emerging talent at The Troubadour, or the dynamic energy of The Roxy Theatre, the city provides a plethora of options to immerse yourself in the enchantment of live music and entertainment.

Ethnic Communities

Los Angeles is a cultural and ethnic melting pot, with each adding to the city's unique tapestry of variety. Exploring the numerous ethnic neighborhoods provides tourists with a one-of-a-kind opportunity to learn about the rich customs, tastes, and cultural history of distinct groups. Here are three ethnic areas in Los Angeles that you should visit:

Olvera Street

Olvera Street in Downtown Los Angeles is known as the "Birthplace of Los Angeles." This ancient Mexican market transports tourists back in time, providing an insight into the city's Mexican history and heritage.

As you go down Olvera Street, you'll notice bright buildings with classic Mexican architecture and beautiful murals. The street is dotted with stores offering Mexican handicrafts, apparel, and souvenirs, making it a perfect location for discovering one-of-a-kind finds.

Authentic Mexican cuisine may be found at the several restaurants and food booths that line the street. Mexico's tastes are plentiful and delicious, from scrumptious tacos and enchiladas to traditional sweets like churros and fresh aguas frescas.

Visit the Avila Adobe, Los Angeles' oldest standing dwelling that has been transformed into a museum reflecting the city's early Mexican-American heritage. Immerse yourself in the colorful Mariachi Plaza, where you can listen to traditional music and watch the year-round cultural festivals.

Koreatown

Koreatown, or K-Town as it is colloquially called, is a lively Central Los Angeles area that is home to one of the largest Korean populations outside of Korea. This bustling enclave provides an enthralling mix of

Korean culture, entertainment, and culinary pleasures.

Explore Koreatown's streets, which are adorned with neon signs and a plethora of Korean businesses such as restaurants, karaoke bars, and beauty salons. Enjoy the tastes of Korean cuisine, which range from scorching barbeque and hearty stews to delectable street food such as Korean fried chicken and savory pancakes.

Discover Koreatown's one-of-a-kind shopping experiences. There's something for everyone, from Korean supermarkets with a vast variety of groceries and snacks to boutique shops selling K-pop items and current apparel.

Koreatown also has multiple jjimjilbang baths and saunas where you may relax and experience traditional Korean bathhouse rituals. These community areas offer a revitalizing getaway from the hustle and bustle of the city, as well as an insight into Korean wellness practices.

Little Tokyo

Little Tokyo, located in Downtown Los Angeles, is a dynamic area that embraces Japanese culture and tradition. When you enter this enclave, you'll be met by historic architecture, lovely gardens, and a sense of calm.

Explore the Japanese American National Museum, which highlights Japanese Americans' history, art, and cultural accomplishments. Visit the Japanese American Cultural & Community Center, which conducts a variety of events and exhibitions throughout the year to showcase the Japanese community's diversity and ingenuity.

Authentic Japanese cuisine may be found at the various restaurants and cafés that line the streets of Little Tokyo. The culinary selections range from sushi and ramen to delectable pastries and matcha sweets and are guaranteed to please your taste buds.

Immerse yourself in the one-of-a-kind shopping experiences available in Little Tokyo. Explore the stores selling traditional crafts, anime, and manga products, and fashionable Japanese clothing. Visit the Weller Court retail complex, which offers a range of Japanese companies ranging from boutiques to bookstores.

Discover the serenity of the James Irvine Japanese Garden, a hidden refuge in Little Tokyo. The skillfully constructed garden provides a tranquil respite as well as an insight into the beauty of Japanese gardening and aesthetics.

Visiting Olvera Street, Koreatown, and Little Tokyo allows you to immerse yourself in the varied cultures and customs that have molded Los Angeles' fabric. These ethnic districts provide a unique view into the city's different populations, urging you to appreciate Los Angeles' cosmopolitan character.

Film and Television Industry

The glamor and glamor of the film and television industries are synonymous with Los Angeles. As the world's entertainment hub, the city allows tourists to travel behind the scenes and immerse themselves in the enchantment of Hollywood. Here are three must-see locations for film and television fans:

Warner Bros. Studio Tour

The studio Warner Bros. The Studio Tour is an exclusive opportunity to tour one of Hollywood's most renowned studios. This interactive experience, located in Burbank, takes you behind the scenes of your favorite movies and TV shows.

You'll get to see working soundstages, backlots, and classic sets during the trip. Explore the renowned Warner Bros. lot, where great films such as "Casablanca" and "The Wizard of Oz" as well as contemporary blockbuster TV programs were shot. Explore the interactive displays that feature props, costumes, and memorabilia from Warner Bros. films.

Don't pass up the opportunity to visit Warner Bros. The Studio Museum, where you can learn about the studio's history and effect on the entertainment business. You could even witness some celebs or a live show in action.

Universal Studios Hollywood

Universal Studios Hollywood is a world-renowned theme park and operating movie studio that immerses guests in the worlds of cinema and television. The park, which is located in Universal City, just north of Hollywood, offers exhilarating rides, live concerts, and behind-the-scenes excursions.

Take the Studio Tour, a tram excursion that takes you across Universal Studios' backlot. You'll get to witness iconic sets, soundstages, and special effects demos, giving you a taste of the magic of filmmaking. The trip also features exciting activities based on popular films like "Jurassic Park" and "The Fast and the Furious."

Rides such as the classic "Jurassic World - The Ride," "Transformers: The Ride 3D," and "The Wizarding World of Harry Potter," where you may experience the beautiful world of Hogwarts, will leave you breathless.

Throughout the day, Universal Studios Hollywood provides live events and entertainment including renowned characters and high-energy acts. There's always something spectacular going on at the park, from action performances to character meet and greets.

Paramount Pictures Studio Tour

The Paramount Pictures Studio Tour provides an intimate look at one of Hollywood's oldest and most significant film studios. The trip takes you around the historic Paramount lot, where innumerable great films and TV episodes have been created. It is located in the center of Hollywood.

During the tour, you'll see the backlots, soundstages, and iconic sets where classic movies and TV shows were shot. Get a behind-the-scenes look at the creativity and skill that goes into producing cinema's enchantment.

Learn about Paramount Pictures' illustrious history and vital contributions to the film business. Through interactive exhibitions and displays, you can learn about the mysteries of iconic movie props and costumes, as well as gain insight into the filming process.

The Paramount Pictures Studio Tour also allows visitors to observe current movies in process, offering a real-time peek into the industry's enthusiasm.

Visiting these locations immerses you in the world of film and television, allowing you to experience the behind-the-scenes magic and Hollywood's rich cinematic past. You'll be immersed in the exciting world of entertainment that has made Los Angeles a worldwide hub for the film and television industry, from visiting renowned studios to experiencing exhilarating rides and live events.

OUTDOOR RECREATION IN LOS ANGELES

Beaches and Coastal Areas

Los Angeles is endowed with beautiful beaches and scenic coastal areas that provide an ideal vacation for outdoor enthusiasts and beach lovers. Whether you want to soak up the sun, participate in water activities, or simply rest by the ocean, Los Angeles' beaches provide something for everyone. The following are three must-see beaches and coastal areas:

Santa Monica State Beach

Santa Monica State Beach, located in the thriving city of Santa Monica, is a popular location with a variety of activities and attractions. The beach spans along the Pacific Ocean for 3.5 kilometers, giving plenty of area for sunbathing, picnics, and beach volleyball.

Take a walk down the famous Santa Monica Pier, which features a Ferris wheel, a roller coaster, and a variety of shops and restaurants. Enjoy the bustling atmosphere as passers-by are entertained by street entertainers. The pier provides breathtaking views of the coastline and is an excellent location for taking unforgettable photographs.

Surfing, paddle boarding, and beachside bike rides are available at Santa Monica State Beach for those seeking more energetic sports. You may hire bikes or rollerblades and ride down "The Strand," a paved walkway that runs parallel to the beach.

Zuma Beach

Zuma Beach, located in Malibu, is recognized for its natural beauty and vast sandy shoreline. This gorgeous beach is popular with both locals and visitors, providing a peaceful respite from the busy metropolis.

Zuma Beach is ideal for swimming and sunbathing, with lifeguards on duty and plenty of parking. The beach is particularly well-known for its fantastic waves, which draw surfers of all skill levels. Even if you're not a surfer, you may enjoy watching experienced surfers catch waves.

Picnic sites with barbecues can be found across the beach, making it an ideal location for a seaside BBQ or a relaxed picnic with family and friends. Take a stroll down the beach and take in the spectacular coastal environment, which includes towering cliffs and stunning rock formations.

Manhattan Beach

This coastal jewel in Manhattan Beach offers a wonderful seaside ambiance as well as a variety of leisure activities. The beach has smooth sand, brilliant blue waves, and a bustling pier that acts as an entertainment center.

Sunbathing, swimming, and beach volleyball are all popular activities on Manhattan Beach. The beach is well-known for its outstanding surfing conditions, with consistent waves attracting both novice and veteran surfers.

Take a stroll around Manhattan Beach Pier, which provides panoramic views of the shoreline and the Pacific Ocean. Learn about local marine life and experience interactive exhibits at the Roundhouse Aquarium, located at the end of the pier.

The neighboring Manhattan Beach Strand is a popular walking, running, and cycling area. Enjoy the scenic views as you walk down the walkway that goes next to the shore, providing vistas of gorgeous coastal residences and the active beach community.

Los Angeles' beaches and coastal areas are ideal for getting outside, whether you want to relax on the sand, catch some waves, or take a stroll along the shoreline. Santa Monica State Beach, Zuma Beach, and Manhattan Beach, with their natural beauty and plethora of recreational activities, provide amazing experiences for beach aficionados and nature lovers alike.

Hiking and Nature

Los Angeles is well-known for its spectacular natural landscapes and hiking paths, in addition to its lovely beaches. Exploring the hiking trails and parks in and around Los Angeles is a must if you're looking for outdoor adventure and a connection with nature. Here are three of the best hiking and natural spots:

Runyon Canyon Park

Runyon Canyon Park, located in the Hollywood Hills, is a popular hiking destination noted for its gorgeous trails and panoramic views of the city. This urban park has hiking pathways for all fitness levels, ranging from short hikes to more difficult uphill treks.

As you climb the paths, you'll be rewarded with views of the Los Angeles cityscape, the Pacific Ocean, and the famed Hollywood Sign. The park is also a renowned site for celebrity sightings and has a dog-friendly atmosphere, making it a popular choice for both residents and visitors.

Aside from hiking, Runyon Canyon Park offers outdoor fitness activities such as yoga classes and group exercises. The park's broad expanses and well-kept pathways provide a great backdrop for a restorative workout in the middle of nature.

Topanga State Park

Topanga State Park is the largest state park inside Los Angeles city boundaries, located in the Santa Monica Mountains. This vast park spans over 11,000 acres of diverse terrain, including rocky canyons, oak woods, and beautiful vistas.

Topanga State Park has a large network of hiking paths with varying levels of difficulty and spectacular views of the surrounding mountains and the Pacific Ocean. The park's pathways allow for exploration, tranquility, and connection with nature.

The renowned Backbone Trail, which spans kilometers and offers a hard and rewarding hiking experience, is one of the park's attractions. Keep an eye out for the different species and colorful wildflowers that add to the park's natural beauty as you trek through it.

Malibu Creek State Park

Malibu Creek State Park, located in the Santa Monica Mountains, is a gorgeous sanctuary with a variety of outdoor activities and magnificent hiking paths. The park's scenery is breathtaking, with rolling hills, oak trees, and the famed Rock Pool, a natural swimming hole situated among lovely surroundings.

Hikers may explore the park's paths, which run through a variety of environments and offer chances for bird watching, animal viewing, and silent introspection. The park also has the well-known MAS*H filming location, where the iconic TV series was filmed, bringing a bit of Hollywood history to your trekking journey.

Malibu Creek State Park, in addition to hiking, includes rock climbing, equestrian riding, and mountain biking, making it a varied location for outdoor lovers. Spend the day in nature, picnicking by the stream or cooling down in the cold waters of the Rock Pool.

Exploring Runyon Canyon Park, Topanga State Park, and Malibu Creek State Park allows you to escape Los Angeles' metropolitan hustle and bustle and immerse yourself in nature's serene splendor. Whether you're looking for a relaxing hike, a strenuous journey, or simply a serene getaway, these locations provide a refreshing outdoor experience that will leave you feeling rejuvenated and inspired.

Sporting Events

Los Angeles is a sports paradise, with a thriving sports culture and a plethora of world-class venues. Attending a game in Los Angeles is an experience not to be missed if you are a sports lover or simply like the thrilling atmosphere of live sporting events. Here are three of the city's most recognizable athletic venues:

Staples Center

Staples Center, located in downtown Los Angeles, is a major sports and entertainment venue that holds a range of events, including basketball and hockey games. It is home to the NBA's Los Angeles Lakers, NBA's Los Angeles Clippers, and NHL's Los Angeles Kings.

Attending a Lakers or Clippers basketball game at Staples Center is a once-in-a-lifetime opportunity to see some of the top players in the NBA in action. Inside the arena, the atmosphere is electrifying, with fervent supporters shouting for their favorite teams.

Catching a Los Angeles Kings game is an opportunity for hockey fans to watch the fast-paced action on the rink and feel the thrill of the NHL.

Throughout the year, Staples Center hosts other big athletic events, concerts, and entertainment performances, making it a vibrant nexus for sports and entertainment in Los Angeles.

Dodger Stadium

Dodger Stadium is a Los Angeles landmark and one of the country's oldest and most historic baseball venues. This renowned ballpark, located in Chavez Ravine, is the home of the Los Angeles Dodgers, one of the most successful teams in Major League Baseball.

Seeing a baseball game at Dodger Stadium is a must-do in Los Angeles. The magnificent background of the San Gabriel Mountains, along with the vibrant mood and fervent support of Dodgers fans, produces an amazing ambiance.

As you cheer on the Dodgers, enjoy classic ballpark snacks like hot dogs and peanuts while learning about the rich history and traditions of America's sport.

Rose Bowl Stadium

The Rose Bowl Stadium, located in Pasadena, is a historic stadium noted for holding significant athletic events, most notably the annual Rose Bowl Game, one of the country's oldest and most prominent college football bowl games.

Attending a football game at the Rose Bowl Stadium allows you to experience the energy and excitement that college football has to offer. The stadium's majestic design, capacity for nearly 90,000 people, and fervent fan base combine to produce an exciting environment that heightens the excitement of the game.

Aside from football, the Rose Bowl Stadium holds several other athletic events, concerts, and even flea markets throughout the year, giving a varied range of activities.

Attending athletic events like Staples Center, Dodger Stadium, and Rose Bowl Stadium allows you to immerse yourself in Los Angeles' vibrant sports culture. These renowned stadiums provide a memorable flavor of the city's sporting skill and enthusiastic following, whether you're a die-hard fan or simply looking to experience the excitement of live sports.

FOOD AND DINING

Local Cuisine and Specialties

Los Angeles is a gastronomic melting pot, with a varied range of flavors and cuisines reflecting the city's culture. From mouthwatering tacos to scorching Korean BBQ to scrumptious food trucks, Los Angeles' local eating culture is sure to fulfill any foodie's needs. Here are three must-try famous local foods and specialties:

Tacos with Mexican Cuisine

Los Angeles is well-known for its vibrant Mexican cuisine culture, with innumerable taco stalls, taquerias, and Mexican restaurants dotting the city. The possibilities range from conventional street tacos to gourmet variants.

To experience true Mexican cuisine, visit the bustling areas of Boyle Heights or East Los Angeles. Try the succulent beef asada tacos, the savory al pastor tacos, or the fresh seafood tacos loaded with shrimp or fish. Don't forget to try the tasty salsas, guacamole, and Mexican street corn (elote).

Explore restaurants that provide modern interpretations of Mexican food for a more premium experience, where you can indulge in inventive delicacies like mole, chiles rellenos, or tamales cooked with unusual ingredients and taste combinations.

Korean Barbecue

Los Angeles, which has a substantial Korean community, is known for its bustling Koreatown, which has an outstanding assortment of Korean BBQ restaurants. Korean BBQ is a hands-on eating experience in which you cook your own marinated meats and serve them with a selection of side dishes.

Visit a Korean BBQ restaurant to enjoy tender and tasty meats such as bulgogi (marinated beef), galbi (marinated short ribs), and samgyupsal (grilled pig belly). Wrap the grilled meat in lettuce leaves, then top with pickled veggies and sauces to create an explosion of tastes and textures.

Korean BBQ is more than simply the meats; it's also about the banchan or little side dishes that complement the meal. Kimchi (spicy fermented cabbage), japchae (stir-fried glass noodles), and savory pancakes are other examples.

Food Trucks

Los Angeles is well-known for its dynamic and diversified food truck culture, which offers a variety of gourmet treats on wheels. These food trucks may be seen all around town, typically congregating in popular places or during major events.

cuisine trucks in Los Angeles provide a diverse range of alternatives, including gourmet burgers and tacos, ethnic street cuisine, and sweet desserts. Korean-Mexican fusion (Kogi BBQ), Filipino food (White Rabbit Truck), and sumptuous dessert trucks (Coolhaus or The Grilled Cheese Truck) are also available.

As these fashionable trucks often travel about the city, look for them at food truck gatherings or on social media. Exploring the Los Angeles food truck culture allows you to indulge in unique and inventive meals while relaxing in a calm outdoor setting.

Local cuisine and specialties of Los Angeles genuinely reflect the city's varied population and culinary influences. Whether you're looking for real tacos on the streets, cooking your meats at a Korean BBQ restaurant, or hunting down the latest food truck hit, Los Angeles has a bustling and interesting culinary culture that will satisfy even the most discriminating palate.

Restaurants & Eateries

Aside from the local food and specialties, Los Angeles is home to numerous notable restaurants and cafes that have become treasured city institutions. From the famous In-N-Out Burger to the renowned diners, these eateries give a flavor of nostalgia as well as a one-of-a-kind dining experience. Here are three notable restaurants and cafes worth visiting:

In-N-Out Burger

No trip to Los Angeles would be complete without a stop at In-N-Out Burger, the iconic fast-food business. In-N-Out Burger has a loyal following of customers who love its excellent burgers, fresh-cut fries, and creamy milkshakes and is known for its basic menu and high-quality ingredients.

Order a traditional Double-Double, which includes two beef patties, two pieces of American cheese, lettuce, tomato, and their distinctive spread, all sandwiched between toasted buns. Add animal-style fries (topped with grilled onions, cheese, and special sauce) and a cool Neapolitan shake to your meal.

In-N-Out Burger embodies the essence of Southern California's laid-back lifestyle with its retro-inspired design and friendly service, making it a must-visit for burger fans.

Original Pantry Cafe

The Original Pantry Cafe in downtown Los Angeles has been providing substantial American breakfasts and classic comfort cuisine since 1924. This historic restaurant is open 24 hours a day, seven days a week, and has become a popular gathering place for both residents and visitors.

Experience the timeless charm of The Original Pantry Cafe. Breakfast selections range from airy pancakes and omelets to hefty dishes of steak and eggs, and are a terrific way to start the day. Enjoy their legendary Pantry Burger, prime rib, or traditional meatloaf for lunch or supper.

The Original Pantry Cafe's no-frills setting, ample quantities, and dependably superb food have helped it become a beloved Los Angeles institution.

Philippe the Original

Philippe the Original, a vintage French dip sandwich establishment in downtown Los Angeles, was founded in 1908. The French dip sandwich, a culinary masterpiece in which thinly sliced roast beef is put in a French roll and dipped in au jus, is said to have originated from this legendary institution.

Step inside Philippe The Original and enjoy the classic atmosphere. Order your French dip sandwich with your choice of meat, such as beef, hog, lamb, or turkey, and specify the amount of juiciness. Serve your sandwich with zesty pickles and one of their classic sides, such as macaroni salad or coleslaw.

Philippe The Original's super sandwiches, long history, and courteous service have earned it a place in the hearts of both residents and tourists.

Visiting these historic restaurants and eateries allows you to immerse yourself in Los Angeles' rich culinary legacy while also indulging in great comfort cuisine that has endured the test of time. Whether it's a burger at In-N-Out, a classic American breakfast at The Original Pantry Cafe, or a French dip sandwich at Philippe The Original, these eateries are an important part of the city's culinary culture.

Food Festivals and Farmers Markets

Los Angeles is known for its robust food culture, and visiting farmers' markets and food festivals is a terrific opportunity to get a taste of the city's culinary scene. These events highlight the finest of Los Angeles' culinary culture, from fresh produce and artisanal items to different cuisines and unique meals. Here are three noteworthy farmers' markets and culinary events to check out:

Hollywood Farmers Market

The Hollywood Farmers Market is a popular location for foodies and residents searching for high-quality, locally-produced products. Every Sunday, this lively market offers a vast variety of fruits, vegetables, artisanal products, baked delicacies, and much more.

Stroll around the vibrant booths, meet farmers and sellers, and sample seasonal fruits and vegetables. Discover one-of-a-kind products such as organic honey, artisanal cheeses, homemade jams, and freshly baked bread. The Hollywood Farmers Market also has food vendors selling great ready-to-eat cuisine, making it ideal for a leisurely breakfast or lunch.

Smorgasburg LA

Smorgasburg LA is a weekly open-air food market that attracts a wide range of food vendors, local chefs, and culinary entrepreneurs. This gourmet destination in Downtown Los Angeles is a must-see for anyone looking for unique and tasty food.

Every Sunday, Smorgasburg LA has a diverse array of food vendors serving everything from worldwide street food to inventive fusion cuisine. Gourmet burgers, handmade tacos, inventive sushi rolls, sumptuous desserts, and much more are available. Local craft brewers, specialty coffee sellers, and live music round out the market's lively and joyful environment.

LA Food Festival

The LA Food Fest is an annual event that highlights Los Angeles' robust culinary industry. This multi-day festival gathers food sellers, celebrity chefs, mixologists, and food lovers from all across the city together. It's a gastronomic festival where participants may try a variety of cuisines and flavors all in one place.

The LA Food Fest features everything from gourmet meals to street food-inspired nibbles, representing Los Angeles' varied gastronomic scene. Cooking demos, live entertainment, and interactive experiences will be available while you sample wonderful cuisine from renowned restaurants, food trucks, and up-and-coming culinary talents.

The LA Culinary Fest is a terrific opportunity to try new cuisines, support local companies, and immerse yourself in Los Angeles' dynamic culinary culture.

Exploring Los Angeles' farmers markets and food festivals delivers a one-of-a-kind and immersive gastronomic experience. Whether walking through the Hollywood Farmers Market, enjoying a broad selection of delicacies at Smorgasburg LA, or attending the LA Culinary Fest, these gatherings provide an opportunity to learn about the city's robust culinary culture and interact with local producers and food aficionados.

NIGHTLIFE AND SHOPPING

Shopping Centers

Los Angeles is a shopper's paradise, with a diverse range of retail areas catering to various styles, preferences, and budgets. The city provides everything for any shopping aficionado, from premium brands and high-end boutiques to contemporary fashion stores and unusual businesses. Here are three prominent retail areas in Los Angeles to visit:

The Rodeo Drive

Rodeo Drive, located in Beverly Hills' premium area, is synonymous with luxury and elegance. This world-famous shopping boulevard is famous for its high-end designer stores, exclusive boutiques, and lavish shopping experience.

Walk along Rodeo Drive and you'll be captivated by the magnificent boutiques that house fashion companies such as Gucci, Prada, Louis Vuitton, and Chanel. Browse through magnificent apparel, accessories, jewelry, and home décor to immerse yourself in the world of luxury. Even if you're not in the mood to purchase, Rodeo Drive's palm-lined avenues, fancy vehicles, and magnificent buildings provide a wonderful environment.

The Grove

The Grove, located in the center of Los Angeles, offers a more accessible and dynamic retail experience. This open-air shopping mall mixes retail therapy with entertainment, making it a popular destination for both locals and tourists.

The Grove features a broad mix of retailers, including well-known names such as Apple, Nordstrom, and Sephora, as well as unusual specialized shops and independent boutiques. Explore the beautifully manicured outdoor mall while looking for the newest fashion trends, unusual gifts, and beauty goods.

The Grove is more than simply a retail mall; it also has a variety of entertainment opportunities. Take in a movie at the Pacific Theatres, listen to live music on the outdoor stage, or ride the lovely trolley that passes through the center. The famed dancing fountain, which comes to life with orchestrated water presentations, should not be missed.

Melrose Avenue

Melrose Avenue is a sanctuary for fashionistas, trendsetters, and people looking for a combination of vintage treasures and current fashions. This busy boulevard in West Hollywood spans many miles and is dotted with an eclectic mix of fashion boutiques, edgy streetwear retailers, vintage shops, and one-of-a-kind galleries.

Explore Melrose Avenue's cutting-edge fashion scene, where you can find new designers, local labels, and one-of-a-kind pieces. Visit vintage apparel, accessories, and antique stores such as Fred Segal, Wasteland, and Melrose Trading Post. Don't miss out on the colorful street art and trendy eateries that contribute to the neighborhood's distinct ambiance.

Melrose Avenue isn't only about fashion; it also has some amazing restaurants. You'll discover a variety of culinary alternatives to satiate your taste buds, from contemporary cafés and food trucks to upmarket restaurants and gourmet diners.

In addition to Rodeo Drive, The Grove, and Melrose Avenue, Los Angeles has a plethora of other shopping districts and neighborhoods worth visiting, including Venice Beach's trendy Abbot Kinney Boulevard, the bustling shopping centers of Westfield Century City and The Americana at Brand, and the diverse mix of stores in the Downtown LA Fashion District.

The retail districts of Los Angeles are more than simply places to buy things; they are experiences in and of themselves. The city's retail areas provide a broad selection of alternatives that appeal to every taste and desire, from strolling down Rodeo Drive and immersing yourself in luxury to discovering unique treasures on Melrose Avenue and enjoying the bustling ambiance of The Grove. So gather your shopping bags and prepare for an unforgettable retail journey in the City of Angels.

Nightlife and Entertainment

Los Angeles is well-known for its thriving nightlife and entertainment scene. The city has a wealth of alternatives for an amazing night out, from fashionable nightclubs and live music venues to comedy clubs and late-night hotspots. Here are three significant nightlife and entertainment districts in Los Angeles:

Sunset Strip

The Sunset Strip is a historic section of Sunset Boulevard in West Hollywood known for its famed nightlife and live music establishments. Since the 1960s, this historic strip has been a center of entertainment, attracting music fans, celebrities, and visitors from all over the world.

Explore the Sunset Strip's diverse venues, which include iconic clubs like The Roxy Theatre, The Whisky a Go Go, and The Viper Room, as well as intimate lounges and bars. These venues have played host to some of the world's finest performers and bands, establishing careers and generating unforgettable musical moments.

Catch a live performance by a new artist or listen to the music of an established group. The Sunset Strip's musical genres and styles span from rock and punk to pop and techno. In one of the city's most renowned nightlife spots, experience the exciting atmosphere, mix with fellow music fans, and dance the night away.

Downtown LA Nightclubs

Downtown Los Angeles has recently been revitalized and has resurfaced as a popular nightlife destination. The neighborhood is home to a plethora of stylish nightclubs, lounges, and pubs that appeal to a wide range of interests and preferences.

Visit the historic Broadway neighborhood, where gorgeous art deco buildings have been turned into chic nightlife spots. Enjoy panoramic views of the city from rooftop bars, dance to the rhythms of renowned DJs in upmarket nightclubs, or chill in quiet speakeasies sipping specialty drinks.

Downtown Los Angeles' nightlife culture is noted for its inventive and fashionable venues that provide one-of-a-kind experiences. Downtown LA has something for everyone, whether you're looking for a refined lounge setting, a vibrant dance floor, or a hidden treasure with a speakeasy ambiance.

Comedy Clubs

Los Angeles is a comedy mecca, and seeing a show at one of the city's famed clubs is a must for anybody looking for a night of laughs. Los Angeles comedy clubs contain both known and developing comedians, giving a venue for laughter and entertainment.

Visit clubs like The Comedy Store, Laugh Factory, and The Improv to see some of the biggest stars in comedy perform. These venues have a long history of launching the careers of many comedians who have gone on to gain renown in the profession.

Prepare to be wowed by funny stand-up routines, improvised humor, and captivating storytelling. The lively energy and intimate environment of comedy clubs offer a one-of-a-kind experience that allows you to connect with the artists and other audience members.

Check the schedules of comedy clubs while visiting Los Angeles, since they frequently offer surprise guest appearances by well-known comedians, adding to the excitement of the night.

Aside from the Sunset Strip, Downtown LA's nightclubs, and comedy clubs, Los Angeles has a diverse nightlife scene that includes themed bars, speakeasies, live music venues, and jazz clubs. The city provides something for every nightlife aficionado, whether you want a bustling party environment or a more quiet setting for discussion and leisure.

Experience the exhilarating excitement of Los Angeles' nightlife, immerse yourself in world-class entertainment, and make amazing experiences as you explore the City of Angels' numerous and dynamic alternatives.

DAY TRIPS AND NEARBY ATTRACTIONS

Hollywood Universal Studios

Universal Studios Hollywood, located only a short drive from the center of Los Angeles, is a must-see site for movie buffs and adrenaline seekers alike. This legendary film studio and theme park provides a one-of-a-kind and immersive experience that allows guests to walk behind the scenes of their favorite movies and TV series.

Explore the backlot of the famed Studio Tour to immerse yourself in the world of entertainment. Experience exhilarating coasters such as the heart-pounding Transformers: The Ride 3D and the adrenaline-pumping Jurassic World - The Ride, as well as sets, soundstages, and iconic locations from popular films such as "Jurassic Park," "King Kong," and "Fast & Furious."

Visit Hogwarts Castle, taste Butterbeer, and fly through the sky on the exciting Harry Potter and the Forbidden Journey experience to immerse yourself in the wonder of The Wizarding World of Harry Potter. Explore Springfield's lively streets in The Simpsons' Springfield USA and join your favorite characters on The Simpsons Ride.

There are also live events, character meet-and-greets, and a variety of food and retail opportunities at Universal Studios Hollywood. A day trip to Universal Studios Hollywood ensures entertainment and excitement for all, whether you're a lover of action-packed blockbusters, family-friendly activities, or immersive experiences.

Disneyland Resort

The Disneyland Resort, located in Anaheim, California, only a short drive from Los Angeles, is a beautiful location that brings fantasies to life. Disneyland Park and Disney California Adventure Park are located within this popular theme park complex.

Enter the magical world of Disneyland Park, where you may explore eight themed zones such as Main Street, U.S.A., Fantasyland, Adventureland,

Tomorrowland, and more. Experience famous rides such as Pirates of the Caribbean, Space Mountain, and It's a Small World. Meet your favorite Disney characters, enjoy enthralling parades, and marvel at breathtaking fireworks displays.

Disney California Adventure Park, located adjacent to Disneyland Park, provides a unique combination of Disney stories and California's colorful atmosphere. Enjoy exhilarating rides such as Guardians of the Galaxy - Mission: BREAKOUT! as well as the Incredicoaster. Explore the amazing Pixar film environments in Cars Land, Toy Story Land, and Avengers Campus. Live concerts, engaging dining experiences, and the brilliant World of Color evening spectacular are all available.

Downtown Disney, an entertainment center with restaurants, shopping, and live entertainment, is also part of the Disneyland Resort. Downtown Disney has something for everyone, from unique eating experiences to exclusive Disney goods.

Catalina Island

A day trip to Catalina Island, a lovely spot located off the coast of Los Angeles, is a great way to get away from the city. Catalina Island provides a peaceful and scenic location, complete with beautiful beaches, crystal-clear oceans, and a relaxed ambiance.

Take a ferry from the mainland to Avalon, Catalina Island's principal town. Discover the picturesque streets teeming with stores, cafés, and art galleries. Relax on the gorgeous beaches, go snorkeling or diving to see the colorful marine life, or climb into the island's interior.

Take a zip line trip to soar over the island's harsh landscape and take in spectacular panoramic views for a thrilling adventure. Take a glass-bottom boat excursion to see the underwater environment, or try kayaking or stand-up paddleboarding.

Catalina Island also provides an opportunity to see animals like dolphins, seals, and bald eagles. Learn about the island's unique environment and participate in educational activities at the Catalina Island Conservancy.

Joshua Tree National Park

A day trip to Joshua Tree National Park is a must for nature lovers and outdoor explorers. This desert wilderness, located east of Los Angeles, is known for its unusual terrain, Joshua trees, and dramatic rock formations.

Explore the park's several hiking paths, which range from casual nature walks to difficult climbs. Admire the rough beauty of Hidden Valley, where rock climbers put their talents to the test on the granite walls. Explore the Cholla Cactus Garden, a one-of-a-kind environment covered with thick clusters of cholla cactus.

Witness beautiful sunsets and stargaze in Joshua Tree National Park's dark sky, which is famed for its superb astronomical conditions. Camping is offered within the park, allowing you to fully immerse yourself in the desert's quiet and natural beauty.

Don't miss out on prominent monuments like Skull Rock and Arch Rock, which highlight the park's unique rock formations. Look for fauna such as bighorn sheep, desert tortoises, and a variety of bird species.

Visit Joshua Tree National Park with caution, as the desert environment may be harsh. To guarantee a safe and pleasurable trip, bring lots of drinks, sunscreen, and proper attire.

The enchantment of amusement parks like Universal Studios Hollywood and Disneyland Resort, as well as the tranquility of Catalina Island and the natural marvels of Joshua Tree National Park, are all available as day trip options near Los Angeles. Whether you're looking for adventure, leisure, or absorption in the world of entertainment, these attractions will make your trip to Los Angeles unforgettable.

USEFUL INFORMATION FOR YOUR TRIP

Accommodations

When visiting Los Angeles, you'll discover a variety of lodging alternatives to fit your interests and budget. Here are several popular options, ranging from luxury hotels to budget-friendly ones:

a. Hotels: There are several hotels in Los Angeles, ranging from world-class luxury lodgings to boutique hotels and budget-friendly corporations. Downtown Los Angeles, Hollywood, Beverly Hills, and Santa Monica are popular destinations to discover hotels that cater to a range of demands.

b. Vacation Rentals: Renting a vacation house or apartment is a popular option for individuals looking for a more intimate and private setting. Websites and platforms such as Airbnb provide a diverse range of residences across the city, allowing guests to experience the comfort and facilities of a home away from home.

c. Hostels: For budget-conscious visitors or those seeking a more social atmosphere, hostels provide inexpensive lodging alternatives. Several hostels in prominent neighborhoods such as Hollywood and Venice Beach provide dormitory-style rooms and shared spaces.

Transportation

Navigating the huge metropolis of Los Angeles may appear overwhelming, but there are a few transit choices available that will allow you to tour the city with ease:

a. Car Rental: For guests who prefer the ease and flexibility of having their transportation, renting a car is a popular option. Several vehicle rental businesses operate offices in and around Los Angeles International Airport (LAX). Be prepared, though, for traffic congestion and restricted parking in certain places.

b. Los Angeles has a large public transit system, mostly buses and railroads. The Metro Rail system, which comprises subway and light rail lines, is operated by the Los Angeles

County Metropolitan Transportation Authority (Metro). The Metro system connects the city's most prominent tourist attractions and districts.

c. Ride-Sharing Services: In Los Angeles, services such as Uber and Lyft are widely available, giving easy transportation alternatives at the touch of a button. Ride-sharing services are a popular option for short-city excursions, and they provide a handy alternative to driving and parking.

d. Bicycles and scooters: The availability of shared bicycles and electric scooters in Los Angeles has increased. Companies like Bird, Lime, and Jump offer bicycle and scooter rentals that may be easily accessible and utilized for short-distance commuting inside the city. When using these services, be careful to acquaint yourself with local rules and safety requirements.

e. Walking: Exploring some districts on foot may be a nice way to see the city, especially in places with pedestrian-friendly streets and nearby attractions. To properly experience the bustling environment, walk down Hollywood Boulevard, Rodeo Drive, and the Venice Beach Boardwalk.

It's critical to organize your transportation alternatives based on your itinerary and the locations you'll be seeing. Los Angeles is notorious for its traffic, so plan ahead of time, especially during peak hours. To make your travel more efficient, consider utilizing navigation applications or examining public transit timetables.

You may make your stay in Los Angeles easier and more pleasurable by picking the most appropriate lodging choice and employing the transportation means that best fit your needs.

Useful Apps and Websites

When visiting Los Angeles, several useful apps and websites can enhance your experience and help you navigate the city:

a. Google Maps: This popular navigation app provides detailed maps, directions, real-time traffic updates, and public transportation information. It can help you plan routes, find nearby attractions, and discover the best transportation options within the city.

b. Metro Trip Planner: The Los Angeles County Metropolitan Transportation Authority (Metro) offers a Trip Planner tool on its website. This tool helps you plan your journey using the Metro Rail and bus systems, providing schedules, fares, and estimated travel times.

c. Uber/Lyft: The Uber and Lyft apps allow you to request rides from drivers in the area. They are convenient for getting around the city, especially if you prefer not to drive or use public transportation.

d. ParkMe/ParkWhiz: These apps help you find parking options in Los Angeles, allowing you to search for available parking spots, compare prices, and even reserve parking in advance.

e. Yelp: Yelp is a popular review platform that can help you find restaurants, cafes, shops, and other businesses in Los Angeles. It provides user reviews, ratings, photos, and detailed information about establishments.

f. Discover Los Angeles (Website): The official website of Discover Los Angeles is a valuable resource for planning your trip. It offers comprehensive information on attractions, events, dining options, and itineraries to help you make the most of your visit.

Customs and Etiquette

To ensure a pleasant and respectful experience during your time in Los Angeles, it's helpful to be aware of some local customs and etiquette:

a. Tipping: It is customary to tip service workers in Los Angeles. In restaurants, it is common to leave a tip of 15-20% of the total bill for good service. Additionally, it is customary to tip hotel staff, taxi drivers, and other service providers.

b. Respect for Diversity: Los Angeles is a diverse and multicultural city, so it's important to respect and appreciate different cultures, languages, and customs. Embrace the city's multicultural atmosphere and be open to experiencing new perspectives.

c. Traffic Etiquette: Traffic can be congested in Los Angeles, so it's important to exercise patience and follow the rules of the road. Be mindful of pedestrians, use turn signals when changing lanes, and avoid aggressive driving behaviors.

d. Respect for the Environment: Los Angeles values environmental sustainability, so it's encouraged to engage in eco-friendly practices. Reduce waste by recycling and conserving resources. Respect natural areas and follow trail guidelines when hiking or exploring outdoor attractions.

e. Dress Code: Los Angeles has a generally casual dress code, but it's recommended to dress appropriately for specific venues or events. When visiting upscale restaurants or clubs, it's advisable to dress smart-casual or by any specific dress code.

f. Personal Space and Boundaries: While Los Angeles is a vibrant and bustling city, it's important to respect personal space and boundaries. Give people sufficient personal space in crowded areas and be mindful of cultural norms regarding personal interaction.

By familiarizing yourself with these practical tips and local customs, you can navigate the city with ease, show respect for the local culture, and have a positive experience during your time in Los Angeles.

CONCLUSION

The City of Angels, Los Angeles, has a dazzling assortment of attractions and experiences to suit a wide range of interests and inclinations. The city is a melting pot of culture, entertainment, and natural beauty, from the flash and glamor of Hollywood to the peaceful coastal moods of Santa Monica and Venice Beach.

Visitors visiting Hollywood may walk the renowned Walk of Fame, see a play at the TCL Chinese Theatre, and gaze out over the city from Griffith Observatory. Downtown Los Angeles entices with its thriving cultural culture, as shown by The Broad and Walt Disney Concert Hall, while the busy Grand Central Market provides a delectable gastronomic journey.

The scenic Santa Monica Pier, Third Street Promenade, and sandy beaches entice visitors to relax and enjoy the traditional California lifestyle. Beverly Hills entices guests with its palatial Greystone Mansion and upscale shopping along Rodeo Drive, while the Getty Center awes with its art treasures and gorgeous architecture.

Venice Beach entices visitors with its quirky promenade, Muscle Beach, and stylish Abbot Kinney Boulevard, while Griffith Park entices nature enthusiasts with its extensive vegetation, observatory, and zoo. Art lovers will enjoy the Getty Center, LACMA, and The Broad, which house treasures from diverse art movements.

The Hollywood Bowl, The Troubadour, and The Roxy Theatre are historic music and entertainment venues with a thriving live music scene. Exploring ethnic districts such as Olvera Street, Koreatown, and Little Tokyo gives visitors an insight into the city's diverse cultural tapestry.

Studio tours at Warner Bros., Universal Studios, and Paramount Pictures provide behind-the-scenes access to the world of entertainment.

The beautiful beaches of Santa Monica, Zuma, and Manhattan Beach, as well as the hiking trails of Runyon Canyon Park, Topanga State Park, and Malibu Creek State Park, will appeal to nature lovers. Staples Center, Dodger Stadium, and the Rose Bowl Stadium all host exciting sporting events.

Los Angeles' culinary culture is a melting pot of different cuisines, with scrumptious tacos and Mexican food, delectable Korean BBQ, and the ever-popular food trucks serving gourmet delicacies.

The city's retail areas, such as Rodeo Drive, The Grove, and Melrose Avenue, appeal to a wide range of interests and budgets, with a diverse selection of high-end boutiques, contemporary businesses, and one-of-a-kind shops.

Los Angeles' nightlife is active and interesting, with the Sunset Strip, downtown LA nightclubs, and comedy clubs delivering memorable evenings of entertainment and enjoyment.

For day excursions and local attractions, Universal Studios Hollywood, Disneyland Resort, Catalina Island, and Joshua Tree National Park are all within a short drive of the city and provide amazing experiences.

Los Angeles delivers a fantastic journey packed with excitement, entertainment, and discovery thanks to its various attractions, dynamic cultural scene, and natural beauty. So, begin your tour, absorb the city's distinct charm, and let Los Angeles enchant you with its limitless possibilities.

Printed in Great Britain
by Amazon

28983703R00077